Princess Mackie BUYS a House

Twala Lockett-Jones

Melissa Bailey
Illustrator

SEASON Press LLC

Published in collaboration with
Fortitude Graphic Design & Printing and Season Press LLC
Funded in part with a grant from the
Arts Council of Greater Kalamazoo
Edited by Maggie Zahrai
Illustrated by Melissa Bailey
Contributed images by Sean Hollins
(pages 23, 33, 37 and 95)
Library of Congress Control Number: 2022905462

ISBN: 978-1-7353600-6-5

Lockett-Jones, Twala
Princess Mackie Buys a House/Twala Lockett-Jones

Summary: *Mackie wishes to one day own her own castle. What
does it take to own a home? Find out with Mackie and her mother
as they work to make their dream come true.*

Printed in the United States of America
1 3 5 7 9 10 8 6 4 2
First Edition

Season Press LLC equips, empowers, and celebrates the
voices of self-published authors.
Seasonpressinc.com

To Mom and Dad
Who instilled the importance of family,
community service, hard work,
education, money management, and
homeownership in all 11 of your
children. Thank you for being my
biggest cheerleaders.

To all the little girls who dream of
having a home with their own
room…and a puppy.

TLJ

Hi! My name is Mackenzie, everybody calls me Mackie...everybody except my mom. She calls me Princess Mackie. You see, my dad gave me that nickname the day I was born because he was so excited to have a little princess.

I have a pretty tiara like a princess. Do you know what else every princess needs? That's right...her very own castle! I have always wanted to live in a castle. But how does a princess get a castle? Let's find out together!

Chapter 1
Mackie's BIG Dream

Mackie loves to DREAM BIG! Her biggest dream is to one day have her very own castle with a bedroom fit for a princess. This dream was planted in her heart by her father from the moment she was born. Each night at bedtime, Mackie's dad would tuck her into bed then tell her a bedtime story. The story would be about the amazing adventures of a beautiful young princess who lived in an enchanted castle.

At the end of the story, Dad would kiss Mackie on the forehead and say, "Always remember, you can do whatever you put your mind to." Then, while extending his pinky finger, he would add, "Promise me you will never stop dreaming, Princess." Mackie would lock pinky fingers with her dad for a "pinky promise" and hug him as tight as she could.

One night, Mackie's father came rushing in from a long day's work just in time to tuck her in for the night. She jumped up from her bed and hurried towards her father who was hiding a surprise behind his back.

"What did you bring me, Daddy?" Mackie said as her dad playfully spun around to keep her from seeing the box.

"I can't hide anything from you, Princess!" He slowly brought the box from behind his back to reveal a beautifully wrapped box with pretty pink ribbons and a large white bow. Mackie and Dad sat on her bed as she ripped off the wrapping paper and lifted the lid off the box. She had never seen anything so incredibly stunning in her whole life. It was a beautiful tiara.

"You can wear this when you get your castle," Dad said. Then he showed her a special message inscribed to Mackie.

Dear Princess,
You can do anything you put your mind to.
Never stop dreaming.
Love Always, Dad

"Oh, Daddy, it's perfect. I LOVE IT! I will cherish it FOREVER!"

Mackie wore her tiara every night as her dad read to her at bedtime in their tiny apartment. At her seventh birthday party, she wore it as her mom took a photo of Mackie and her dad. A few months after her birthday, Mackie's father became very ill. Sadly, he passed away and it broke her heart.

Every time she put on her beautiful tiara, she smiled and remembered the birthdays, bedtime stories, and other special moments they shared. The tiara reminded Mackie of the pinky promise she made to her dad to never stop dreaming.

Mackie and her mom continued to live in their apartment not far from downtown. On the first day of each month, Mackie brought the rent downstairs to Mr. and Mrs. Ollie. She was quite fond of the Ollies because they remind her of her own grandparents who lived far away. They were the **landlords** who had owned the building for more than 50 years. When their children grew up and moved away, they turned the upstairs into an apartment.

"One, two, buckle my shoe. Three, four, shut the door," Mackie sang as she bounced down each wooden stair.

Before she could get to the bottom of the stairs, Mrs. Ollie's door swung open. "Heavens, child! I can hear you upstairs thumping and bumping all around. What are you doing up there?"

"I'm sorry, Mrs. Ollie! I try to be real quiet, but sometimes I just can't help it," Mackie giggled.

Mrs. Ollie smiled and her rosy cheeks made her plump round face glow like a ripe peach. "Okay, Mackie, I accept your apology...again!"

Mrs. Ollie went inside her apartment to write a receipt to show the rent had been paid. "Now, take some of my famous cookies to share with your mom. And, Mackie... PLEASE try to keep quiet!"

"Yes, Ma'am. Thank you!" Mackie said as she bounced up each of the fifteen stairs back to her apartment. Mrs. Ollie threw up her arms and laughed.

***

Mom agreed to allow Mackie one of Mrs. Ollie's delicious cookies before dinner. She munched on it at her desk while drawing a picture of her dream princess room. Mackie loved living on Elm Street, but she wished she had her OWN castle.

"Look at this room," Mackie said to her dolls. "It has pink walls with sparkles on the ceiling. If I had this room, I could play, dance, paint the walls and even hang pictures. I could decorate however I want."

Mackie neatly pinned her beautiful picture to her dream board so she could look at it every day. "I wish I had a room like this," she sighed. Her meeting with her toy friends ended when Mom called out, "Princess...dinner is ready!"

Mackie felt so inspired by her picture that she decided to dress in her best princess dress

and wear her precious tiara to dinner. She carefully removed her tiara from the satin pink box her father gave her. She neatly set the tiara around her ponytail puffs and grabbed the picture from her dream board.

"Mommy, can we PLEEEEEEASE make me a princess room like this one? Please, please, pretty please?"

"Well…good evening to you, too, Princess," Mom said as she held out her arms for Mackie to come close for a kiss. "Don't you look pretty!"

"Sorry, Mom. Good evening, my Queen," Mackie said as she curtsied like a princess. "Can you please make me a princess room like this one?"

Mom returned the curtsy and smiled. When Mackie held up her dream board her mom was impressed.
"Wow! This room is amazing, Princess. You are a very talented artist. But, I'm so sorry. We can't paint the walls or glue stars and glitter on the ceiling because we don't own this apartment. We are **tenants** here and the Ollies' have rules about painting or nailing anything on the walls."

"What's a tenant?"

"A tenant is someone who pays rent to live in a house or apartment that is owned by someone else," Mom said.

"Well...I don't want to be a tenant. I want to be a REAL princess with my OWN castle!"

Mom gently squeezed Mackie's cheek. "But, sweetie, you are a real princess. You're Mommy's little princess, remember?"

"Mom, if I'm a princess, that makes you a queen, right?"

"Yes, Sweetie, that's right. You are a princess and I am a queen. We are royalty," Mom said as she pretended to hold a royal gown between her fingers and curtsy.

"Well...if I'm a princess, and you are a queen, then we should have our OWN castle! All the princesses in my books have castles, so why can't we?"

Mom turned away from her daughter's sad face and washed the dishes. She didn't know what to say. She wished she could give her daughter a beautiful princess room like the one Mackie had drawn.

Mackie tried to hold back her tears as she removed the tiara from her head and placed it on the kitchen table. "Mommy, I don't want to be called Princess Mackie until I have my very own castle. I wish Daddy was here. He would get us a castle." Mackie gazed at her tiara through tears.

"You will always be my princess," Mom said.

Mackie picked up the tiara, pushed her chair back and left the table without finishing her dinner. She moped back to her room, , and tossed it onto a box. She didn't think of the pinky promise she made with her father. She had lost hope of ever getting her castle.

Mom finished washing the dinner dishes without her usual help from Mackie. She knew Mackie's feelings were hurt. *Mackie is right. Kings and queens own territory. They have kingdoms and own land.*

She began to wonder what kind of legacy she was building for Mackie. She remembered the conversations with Mackie's dad about buying their first home so Mackie could have a puppy and a princess room. *Now is the time*, Mom said to herself. *But how?*

That night, Mom and Mackie lay across

11

Mackie's bed and dreamed of how wonderful it would be to own their own home. Mackie wanted a home where she could dance as much as she wanted. She would have a backyard to run freely with a fluffy puppy.

Mom wanted Mackie to have room for slumber parties where the girls could be as loud as they pleased. Mom wanted her own garden to grow vegetables and pretty flowers for the bees and butterflies to enjoy.

The hopes and dreams made Mackie sleepy. Mom kissed her on the forehead. "Goodnight, Princess."

As Mom got up from the bed, Mackie extended her pinky finger just like her dad used to do with her. "Mom, promise me you will never stop dreaming."

Mom wrapped her pinky around Mackie's and smiled. "Pinky promise."

CHAPTER 2
The BIG First Step

The next morning, Mom and Mackie had an extra pep in their steps as they walked down Elm Street to the park downtown. Mackie was always excited to see her best friend Braxten for their playdate. But today Braxten and his parents noticed Mackie and her mom smiling brighter than usual. They were even humming a happy tune.

"Well, well, well! What's got you two so excited?" asked Braxten's mom, Olivia.

"We're buying a castle!" Mackie blurted out, then quickly slapped her two hands over her mouth as if she had revealed their big secret.

"Whoaaaa! Wayyyy cool!" Braxten said and

gave his friend a high-five.

"Mackie and I spent the whole night talking and dreaming of a house of our own," Mom said. "I think it's finally time for me to take the BIG step. I'm excited and scared at the same time. I have been a renter my whole life, and I have no idea where to begin."

"How exciting! I know exactly how you feel," Olivia said as she gave Mackie's mom a hug. "We just bought our first home last year." Your first step should be a visit to the Neighborhood Homeownership Center. They have tons of information and classes for first-time homebuyers. They even offer classes on how to care for and maintain your home."

"Oh! I didn't even think of the work that would be needed on the home without the help of a landlord. Wow. That gives me a lot more to think about," Mom said.

"Don't worry," Olivia said. "We learned to fix what we could and how to find trustworthy and dependable **contractors** to fix what we couldn't. It's worth it! We LOVE being homeowners because it gives us ownership in our community and a chance to make a difference."

Braxten's dad, Tom, agreed and added that owning a home gives owners a lot of options. "We can sell it and make a **profit**, or we can **borrow** money against the **equity** in the home. But our plan is to pay off our home and pass it on to this little guy someday. A home is a great way to build **generational wealth**."

"Yea! Pops said I'm going to be very wealthy when I grow up, so I'd better learn how to handle it," Braxten said, poking out his chest in pride.

Everyone laughed. Tom ruffled Braxten's hair then motioned for the kids to run so he could toss them a ball.

"That is EXACTLY what I want for my Mackie," Mom said with new confidence.

The parents sat on a park bench and continued to talk about homeownership while Mackie and Braxten played with their friends.

***

Early the next morning, Mom called the local Neighborhood Homeownership Center

and made an appointment to meet with a homeownership specialist. She was told to bring proof of how much she makes at work, her bank account statements, rent receipts, and income tax returns.

"Whew, that's a lot of information!" she said to the receptionist.

"Yes, this is a BIG step," the receptionist responded in a kind and reassuring tone. "Homeownership is life-changing, so it's a bit of a process. We look forward to seeing you tomorrow!"

When Mom hung up the phone, she was excited and a bit nervous. "Yes...this is a big step, but I can do this," she whispered.

CHAPTER 3
The BIG Roadmap to Homeownership

Mom picked Mackie up from school and the two drove to the Neighborhood Homeownership Center. She wanted Mackie to be a part of every step in making their dream come true. Mackie learned that her grandparents and many of her relatives were renters. So this was a new, big step for the both of them. Even though Mom had some doubts and fears, she was determined to be the first homeowner among them.

When they walked into the Center, Mom took a deep breath. She hoped she had all of the correct information the receptionist had asked her to bring. While Mom was nervous, Mackie

boldly marched right up to the receptionist with a big smile on her face. "Hello, my name is Mackenzie, but everybody calls me Mackie. We want to buy a house."

"Hello, beautiful!" the receptionist said as she gave Mackie a lollipop. "I will let Mr. Collins know right away that there is a Miss Mackie here to see him."

Mr. Collins came out and shook Mackie and Mom's hands. Mackie tried not to laugh at his funny mustache that stretched across his face and curled up on the ends like a smile.

"Hi, sir," Mackie said, shaking his hand. "My name is Mackenzie, but everybody calls me Mackie. We want to buy a castle!"

Mr. Collins chuckled. "Well, follow me, little lady, and let's see what we can do."

He collected all of Mom's information and asked her to fill out a few forms so he could see her **credit report** history. He shared a lot of good information and gave them a "To Do" list that he called homework. Mackie giggled because all of a sudden she wasn't the only one with homework.

The list included paying off a few old bills.

Mom was embarrassed because she hadn't always made the best financial decisions in the past. Some of those old bills she had totally forgotten about.

"Don't worry. This happens from time to time," Mr. Collins said to make Mom feel better. "It's never too late to own up to your debts and pay them to show you are responsible with your money. A good payment history shows the **lender** that you will keep the promise of a **mortgage**."

The last paper Mr. Collins handed Mom was bright and pink. At the top it read, "9 Simple Steps to Buying Your First Home."

"This is your road map to homeownership," Mr. Collins said while twisting the end of his funny mustache. "So buckle up and get ready! Just follow the road map and be sure to check each box as you complete the steps along the journey."

He told Mom that the steps were simple, but not always easy. "There may be times when you want to give up," he said. "But stay focused, work hard, make some sacrifices, and you WILL become a homeowner!"

9 Simple Steps to Buying Your First Home

☐ Step 1: Save Money for Your Down Payment

☐ Step 2: Get Pre-Approved for a Mortgage

☐ Step 3: Find the right Real Estate Agent

☐ Step 4: Shop for the Right House.

☐ Step 5: Make an Offer

☐ Step 6: Have a Home Inspection

☐ Step 7: Get a Home Appraisal

☐ Step 8: Closing Day!

☐ Step 9: MOVE IN!!! CONGRATULATIONS! You're a Homeowner!

CHAPTER 4
The BIG Savings Challenge!

Part of the homework was to attend homeownership workshops. Each week, Mr. Collins taught future home buyers the **"9 Simple Steps to Buying Your First Home."**

Week One
Step 1: Save for Your Down Payment

Mr. Collins kept repeating, "Save, Save, Save!" He had each person create a **budget**. Mackie laughed because he said the budget would help Mom tell her money what to do.

"How can you talk to money?" she snickered.

Then he explained, "A budget is simply telling your money what to do instead of wondering where it went."

"Oh, that's how to talk to money," Mackie said softly.

Mr. Collins walked to the board and asked the class to share ways they could save extra money. "I save spare change, even pennies I find on the ground," one participant shared. "I saved over $300 in loose change last year!"

"Couch money," Mr. Collins wrote.

Couch Money

"Well, I have a lot of stuff I no longer need, and my kids have outgrown a lot of clothes, shoes, and toys. I could have a yard sale," another participant said.

Yard Sale

"Excellent!" Mr. Collins said enthusiastically as his marker screeched on the board. "Keep 'em coming, folks, we need that down payment money!"

"I set aside $3,000 from my tax refund to jumpstart my savings toward a house!" Mom shouted.

"Wow! That's a fantastic idea!" Mr. Collins said as he wrote "Tax Money is YOUR MONEY!!" in big green letters.

Tax Refund

Mackie raised her hand. "OOOh, OOOh! I'll walk the neighbors' dogs, and I'll stop asking to go to the Burger Barn so often!"

The future homeowners chuckled and Mr. Collins invited Mackie to write "Cut Back on Eating Out" and "Walk Dogs" on the board. "That's awesome! Thank you, Mackenzie! Hard work and sacrifice includes ALL OF US, even the children."

The ideas came as fast as Mr. Collins could write.

Save tax refund

Cancel cable TV & magazine subscriptions

Save spare change

Have a yard sale

Eat out less often

Walk dogs

Babysit on the weekends

Rake leaves/ shovel snow for neighbors

Clip coupons

Get a second job

Mom quickly realized how many ways she could cut back on spending to earn extra money for the down payment. Everyone left the first workshop energized and excited.

The next day, Mom and Mackie put their plan into motion. They opened a special savings account at their bank and nicknamed it "Mackie's Castle Fund." Their first deposit was $10. Mom knew it did not seem like much, but it was a start.

On the drive home, Mom said, "Honey, I know how much you love those burgers and chocolate shakes from the Burger Barn. So if you're willing to make such a huge sacrifice, I will prepare my lunch for work AND make my own coffee instead of spending $5 for a cup at the coffee shop every morning. Deal?"

Deal!" Mackie agreed as they shook hands.

The four weeks of classes seemed to fly by. They had reviewed everything from preparing to purchase their first home to, more importantly, how to KEEP up with mortgage payments and home repairs. On the last day of class, Mr. Collins gave every participant a giant piece of paper and a red marker.

The paper had a large thermometer printed on it. He instructed everyone to write their **down payment** goal at the top of the thermometer, then use the red marker to track how much they had saved toward their goal. Mackie loved the idea.

Mackie's job was to color in the thermometer each time they made a deposit into the Castle Fund. Being able to see the thermometer rise kept them excited and motivated.

"Mommy, I want to use the money I've been saving for a puppy to help us buy our castle."

Mom was speechless. She knew how much Mackie loved puppies and how badly she wanted one of her own. "Honey...I can't let you do that. You've been saving that money for such a long time."

"The faster we get a house, the faster I can have a puppy."

"Ok, Princess, that makes perfect sense!" Mom said and gave Mackie a big hug and a kiss on her cheek. "You are wise beyond your years, young lady."

Mackie began to look at the houses in her community differently than ever before. Each one in her historic neighborhood was beautiful and unique in its own way. Many of the houses were more than 100 years old. Mackie especially loved the **Victorian home** directly across the street from their apartment. She often admired it from her bedroom window.

Mrs. Robinson lived in that huge house all by herself. She was a quiet older woman. Her children were all grown up and had families of their own. Mrs. Robinson was rarely home because she often traveled to spend time with her children and grandchildren in other cities.

She enjoyed sitting on her front porch on warm days and waving to the neighbors as they passed by. Mackie always smiled and said, "Hello." Mackie was told not be a bother to Mrs. Robinson, so she was careful to follow her mother's instructions.

CHAPTER 5
The BIG Mortgage Loan Pre-Approval

Mom and Mackie did everything they could all winter to save up money for their down payment. Mom paid off some old bills so her **credit report** looked great. Mackie eagerly finished coloring the last spot at the top of the thermometer Mr. Collins had given them to keep track of their savings goal. They could now check off:

Step 1: Save Money for Your Down Payment

STEP 1: Save Money for a Down Payment.

They finally were ready to meet with Mrs. Lopez. She was one of the mortgage loan officers on a list of mortgage lenders provided by the Homeownership Center. On a beautiful spring morning, they took a stroll from home to their neighborhood bank. When Mrs. Lopez greeted them with a smile Mackie immediately noticed something that made her giggle. Mrs. Lopez had a gap in her teeth just like Mackie.

"Come on in," Mrs. Lopez said as she ushered them into her office. The mother and daughter had been inside the bank a million times to cash checks or make deposits, but they had never met with the mortgage loan officer. Mrs. Lopez collected all of Mom's information from the "homework" checklist from Mr. Collins. They discussed different types of mortgage loan products, down payment requirements, and closing costs.

Mom had learned in the homeownership class that it was important to research and compare other lenders' rates and fees. Mackie was so proud to see her mom **negotiate** for

a better **interest rate** and lower fees on a mortgage loan. Mrs. Lopez' slim fingers danced around her calculator as she added, subtracted, added some more, and then multiplied and divided. Whew! Mackie thought as she looked on in amazement.

Finally, Mrs. Lopez looked over the top of her glasses. "You've done a great job. You both should be very proud of your hard work. Your credit score has improved and you have saved up a sufficient down payment."

Just as quickly as she had punched keys on the calculator, she tapped away at the keyboard. "Save, click, and...print," she sang and then rolled her chair across the office to her printer. She picked up the paper, scribbled her name on the bottom, and handed it to Mom.

Mom's eyes began to water and she grabbed a tissue from the box on the desk.

"What's wrong, Mom?"

Mom couldn't bring herself to talk. She turned the letter to Mackie so she could read the bold letters that read:

**Congratulations! YOU ARE
PRE-APPROVED TO BUY A HOME!**

Step 1: Save Money for Your Down Payment ☑
Step 2: Get Pre-Approved for a Mortgage ☑

Mackie jumped up from the big comfy office chair and leapt into her mother's arms. "YAY! "I'm getting a castle...I'm getting a castle!"

Mom wiped her tears of joy and thanked Mrs. Lopez for the good news.

The soon-to-be homeowners danced and clapped their hands as they seemed to float down the street toward home. Those who passed by them were amused at the duo who sang, "We're getting a castle, we're getting a castle!"

When they arrived home, Mackie rushed to the list on the refrigerator. She took the red marker and checked off the box that read:

STEP 2: Get Pre-Approved for a Mortgage.

Mackie was excited. "Now we need to do the next step:

STEP 3: Find a Real Estate Agent.

Her mom remembered a woman from church who had given her a business card. She pulled her wallet from her purse and found the card for Mrs. Holmes, a local real estate agent. "I will call Mrs. Holmes this weekend to set up a meeting."

CHAPTER 6
The BIG "Castle" House

As Mackie and Braxten walked home from school, they saw two men carrying furniture and boxes out of the house across the street from Mackie's apartment. The men were loading the items into a big white truck that read: Bob's Moving Service. The moving men were big, sweaty, and looked tired.

"Excuse me, sir, what's going on?" Mackie asked one of the men helping carry a huge sofa to the truck.

"All we know is someone is moving out, kid. We just pack 'em up and move 'em out," he said as he struggled to lift his side of the couch onto the truck.

Mackie stared at the men as they moved furniture, refrigerators, and boxes of clothing onto the truck. For the first time, she looked at the house in a different way. She always had thought the house was cute with its flower garden and colorful window shutters. But this was the very first time she noticed that it looked like…a castle.

Mackie and Braxten rushed across the street toward her apartment, raced up all fifteen steps, and burst into the kitchen. "Mom! Mom!" Mackie shouted.

"Guys, remember Mrs. Ollie lives downstairs. Please keep it down."

"But, Mom, there is a moving van at Mrs. Robinson's house!"

"Really? I knew Mrs. Robinson was planning to live with her daughter, but I didn't know she was moving this soon. Good for her."

"Maybe she will sell the castle to us, Mommy!" Mackie said jumping up and down.

Mom had forgotten all about the noise Mackie and Braxten were making as they jumped in excitement. She was a bit excited too. "Well, anything is possible, Princess. I've never been inside Mrs. Robinson's home, but I love the look of it from the outside."

"I love it too, Mommy! It looks just like a castle for a princess!"

Mom smiled. The castle house was cute, she thought. She was so excited she asked Braxten to stay for dinner.

"Yes, ma'am, tacos are my favorite!" Braxten said rubbing his tummy and nodding his head. "I'll call my mom to let her know."

During dinner, Mackie and Braxten chatted about all the things Mackie could do if she owned the castle house. When Braxten left for home, Mom and Mackie began to wash the dishes. They dreamed out loud about how the castle might look inside.

Were the rooms big?

Did it have high ceilings?

Were there lots of cupboards?

And, most importantly...did it have a bedroom fit for a princess?

CHAPTER 7
The BIG House Tour

The next day, Mackie and Braxten counted the money they had earned from walking the neighborhood dogs. They had $15 to add to the Castle Fund. As they neatly placed the money into an envelope, Mackie noticed a well-dressed man who placed a "FOR SALE" sign in the front yard of Mrs. Robinson's castle house. And just as fast as he appeared, he jumped in his car and whisked away.

"Braxten, I will see you later," Mackie said as she raced up the stairs and burst into the kitchen. "Mommy! Mommy! The castle across the street is for sale!" She grabbed her mother's hand and pulled her toward the living room window. "See? For Sale," Mackie pointed. "Can we please go see it? Please?"

"Whoaaaaaa! Hold your horses, Sweetheart. I'll call Mrs. Holmes to schedule an appointment to tour the house." Mom fumbled through her wallet for Mrs. Holmes' business card. When she called, she learned that Mrs. Holmes was already in the neighborhood. She had just finished a **showing** at a different house and could meet them at the castle house in ten minutes.

Mom was just as excited as Mackie. She quickly turned off the stove to put dinner on hold, washed her hands, and replaced her apron with her jacket. They both rushed down the stairs, forgetting Mrs. Ollie's quiet-on-the-stairs rule, and sat on the front steps to wait.

***

A few minutes later, a woman pulled her shiny car into the driveway. Mackie was impressed with the agent's stylish red suit and shiny red high heels. Mom smiled and waved. It was Mrs. Holmes, a lady Mackie recognized

from church. They hurried across the street just as Mrs. Holmes arrived at the front door of the castle.

"Excuse me, Miss! EXCUSE ME, MISS!" shouted Mackie while waving her arms to make sure the lady noticed them. By the time they made it across the street Mackie was out of breath. In between huffs and puffs, Mackie introduced herself.

"Hello, ma'am. My name is Mackenzie, but everybody calls me Mackie. We would like to buy this castle, please."

The woman chuckled and shook her hand. "Hello there, beautiful. It's very nice to meet you. My name is Mrs. Holmes and I own Hometown Realty."

"Can you help me and my mommy buy this castle?" Mackie said, still catching her breath.

Mom shook hands with Mrs. Holmes and reminded her that they had met a while ago at church. "I kept your card in my wallet all this time. Honestly, I never imagined I would need it. We are pre-approved to purchase a home and we would love for you to be our real estate agent."

"I would love to represent you as your **buyer's agent**. A buyer's agent guides the buyer through the home purchase."

Mrs. Holmes pointed to the "For Sale" sign that had a smiling man standing next to a house. She said that was Jim Smith, from Uptown Realty. He is the **seller's agent**. His job is to let people know that the seller's house was available to buy. They learned that Mrs. Robinson could no longer manage the big house on her own and had moved in with her daughter and grandchildren.

"So can you help us buy this castle?" Mackie interrupted. "You see, ma'am, we must buy this castle because my mommy calls me Princess Mackie, but I can't be a real princess until we have our very own castle… ALL the princesses in my books live in beautiful castles," she said without taking a breath.

"Absolutely, Miss Mackie, I would love to work with you."

Mrs. Holmes pulled a Buyer's Agency contract from her binder. It explained all she would do to help them. She pulled another piece of paper from her binder and quickly wrote, "Miss Mackie is hiring Mrs. Holmes, the real estate agent, to find a castle fit for a princess. Miss Mackie hereby agrees to take good care of her new home." She added a line for Mackie to sign and date. Mom and Mackie reviewed and signed their contracts.

"Well, I guess that makes you my boss, Mackie! How would you like to join me right now for a tour, boss?"

Mackie loved being called the boss. Before Mom could say anything, Mackie was already running toward the front door. As soon as Mrs. Holmes turned the key and unlocked the door, Mackie flew past her like a rocket.

Her big bright eyes and mouth were wide with amazement. For the first time since she uttered her first word, Mackie was speechless. Her eyes gazed at stairs that seemed to wind up into the sky. The huge crystal chandelier glowed from the sun's rays and created a sea of rainbows that danced throughout the room.

After staring at the crystals, she snapped out of it and dashed up the never-ending staircase. She didn't bother to look at the kitchen, the dining room, or the living room. Mackie was on a mission! "Where is my princess room?" she said to herself.

At the top of the stairs was a long hallway. There were two doors on the left, one on the right, and one straight ahead. She opened the first door on the left. There was a small bedroom with blue walls and blue carpet and a plain wooden desk in the corner. *Blah...boring,* she thought, and continued on her mission.

She opened the next door but it was just the bathroom. "Nice and clean, yes, but this was definitely NOT a princess room!" she said as she closed the door and skipped down the hall toward the next door. She turned the knob, the door squeaked. Mrs. Holmes and Mom were right behind her as she opened the door.

"Wow!" Mom said. "This room is huge! And look, the flower wallpaper looks like a flower garden exploded all over the walls."

Mrs. Holmes grinned and said, "This is the primary bedroom. The one who pays the mortgage gets the largest room!"

Mackie didn't mind one bit that it would be her mother's room. Mrs. Holmes led the way to the last door. Mackie took a deep breath as she turned the glass knob. The tiny invisible hairs stood on Mackie's arms. She closed her eyes and repeated, "PLEASE, PLEASE, PLEASE, be my princess room!"

The heavy wooden door creaked and brushed across the carpet. Mackie stepped across the threshold into the room and opened her eyes slowly. On the outside, she was as still as a cemented cherub statue. But on the inside, there were fireworks!

"THIS. IS. THE. EXACT. ROOM. OF. MY. DREAMS!" she squealed.

Mackie's eyes slowly and carefully scanned the room. She admired the pretty shade of pink on the walls. And the thought of having her very own stunning chandelier in her bedroom was beyond her wildest dreams. The curtains seemed to have been made from a true royal princess gown as their elegance shone in the sunlight.

There was a large white rug with fancy silver threads that shimmered under the light. With each step Mackie took on the carpet, the fancy silver threads danced and swayed.

"Mom, do you see this bed?" Mackie said

in awe. "THE BED! OH MY GOODNESS, THE BED!" she said over and over again. This was the dream bed Mackie had drawn for her dream board. It had a canopy and sheer white fabric gathered at each bedpost tied with a big beautiful bow.

"It's perfect!" Mackie's voice ripped through the room. She spun herself around and collapsed onto the bed as if to faint. She was being extra dramatic. "Oh, Mommy, we MUST buy this home! It is everything I've always dreamed about!"

This is the one, Mom thought. *This is our future home.* Mom held back tears. She wished she could have shared this moment with Mackie's father. It had been their dream to own a home and raise their family together.

"If you are willing to work with us, we would really like to buy this house and make it our home," Mom said. She showed Mrs. Holmes the pre-approval letter from Mrs. Lopez, the mortgage loan officer. It showed the amount they could afford.

"Based on the pre-approval amount, you can afford to purchase this house," she said, smiling directly at Mackie.

Mom's emotions went from excitement to fear. Mrs. Holmes tried to make her feel better.

"Don't worry, your emotions are perfectly normal. My role as your Buyer's Agent is to be there with you every step of the way. I will look out for your best interest. This is one of the largest investments you will ever make. It is important that you feel you are making the best choice. So I would like to show you a few more homes before you make your final decision."

Mom and Mackie agreed to look at other homes, but they couldn't imagine anything more perfect than this castle.

***

The two were ready to check:

STEP 4: Shop for the Right House.

But they agreed to allow Mrs. Holmes to show them more homes. The next day, Mrs. Holmes met Mackie and Mom at a house across town. Mackie noticed that all the houses on the street looked the same. The inside of the home was nice and neat, but it did not look like a castle. There was no dreamy staircase, no sparkly chandelier, and no princess room. As they walked through each room of the home they did not feel the same excitement they felt in the castle house.

They spent the rest of the day touring one home after another until, finally, an exhausted Mackie yawned, "I don't want to see any more houses. We want the castle house."

Mom agreed. "Thank you for taking the time to show us so many nice homes today, but we feel the castle house is the best one for us. We would like to make an offer."

"That's great!" Mrs. Holmes said, clapping her hands. "Since this is such a big and important decision, and you both are clearly tired, spend the night thinking about your offer and we will complete and sign the paperwork tomorrow." They all agreed.

CHAPTER 8
The BIG Offer

Mom and Mackie woke up early, ate breakfast, and got dressed to meet with Mrs. Holmes. They prepared the **offer** using a form called a **purchase agreement**. They were ready for:

STEP 5: Make an Offer.

This form had blanks that were filled in to list the address of the new home, the offer amount, the date they would like to **close** the deal, and other important information about the property. After they completed the offer, Mom signed her name in the same fancy cursive scribble that she always used on Mackie's field trip forms for school.

"That's it! Now I will present your offer to the seller and I will have a response for you tomorrow morning," Mrs. Holmes said.

For the rest of the day, Mom and Mackie could think about nothing else. Mackie laughed as she put her shoe on the wrong foot. And Mom added salt to her coffee instead of sugar. Both of them were excited and could barely wait to hear back on their offer.

***

The next morning, the phone rang as Mackie and Mom ate breakfast. The two looked at one another and smiled. Mom took a deep breath and answered. It was Mrs. Holmes. Mom put the phone on speaker so Mackie could listen.

"I have news about your offer. Is now a good time for me to stop by?" Mrs. Holmes asked. Mom couldn't tell by her voice if she wanted to share good news or bad news.

"Ah, sure, of course. We will see you soon," Mom said as she looked at Mackie. When she hung up the phone, neither of them said a word.

Several minutes later, Mackie heard high heels coming up the stairs. She flung the door open to see Mrs. Holmes before she could even ring the doorbell.

"Good morning, boss," Mrs. Holmes greeted Mackie with a big smile and a wink.

Mackie ushered Mrs. Holmes into the kitchen where Mom sat at the table nervously fidgeting with the bracelet on her wrist. Mom offered Mrs. Holmes some tea and offered her a seat. Right away, Mrs. Holmes began to share that many people were interested in Mrs. Robinson's home. There were several offers on the home. Mom's head hung down in disappointment.

"But," Mrs. Holmes added, "I have great news. Mrs. Robinson has accepted YOUR offer!"

Mom was speechless, but Mackie had plenty of words for them both.

"Thank you, Mrs. Holmes! You are the BESTEST real estate lady in the whole world!" She gave Mrs. Holmes a tight hug.

Mom and Mrs. Holmes discussed:

STEP 6: Have a Home Inspection.

Mrs. Holmes provided a list of several good home inspectors for Mom to choose from. While Mrs. Holmes went over some final details with Mom, Mackie disappeared to her bedroom.

She returned holding an envelope.

"Can you please give this letter to the seller? I sprinkled it with fairy dust." She handed Mrs. Holmes the envelope neatly decorated with glitter and hearts. Mrs. Holmes admired the pretty artwork and agreed to deliver the beautifully decorated message.

Mom thanked Mrs. Holmes again and walked her to the door. Before Mrs. Holmes could get down the stairs, Mom and Mackie began to dance around the kitchen singing, "We're going to live in a castle, we're going to live in a castle."

Dear Mrs. Robinson,

It's me, Mackie. I am the little girl who lives across the street with my mom. Thank you for choosing our offer to buy your house. We really love it! It is very beautiful! It looks just like a castle and the bedroom is perfect for a princess like me. I promise we will take very good care of it.

Love,

Princess Mackie

CHAPTER 9
The BIG Inspections

Mom called Mr. Chester, the **home inspector**. He was one of the people on the list Mr. Collins shared during homeownership class. Mr. Chester checked EVERYTHING inside and outside of the castle house. One moment he was climbing on the roof then he was down the chimney like Santa Claus.

Next, he crawled through the attic, then he ran the water for about an hour to check for leaks. He flickered lights throughout the house and checked the outlets. He even made sure the foundation of the house was solid and strong. Finally, he searched the entire house for creepy crawly bugs, and Mackie was right beside him

at every turn.

"I'm looking for termites and carpenter ants," he said, smiling as if he were searching for gold. "They love to chew on wood and those little creepy-crawlies can destroy an entire house."

"Yuck! We definitely don't want those greedy bugs to eat our house!" Mackie said, shaking her head vigorously. "Absolutely NOT!"

Mr. Chester dusted himself off, put his flashlight in his toolbox, and checked some final things on his list. Mom saw him writing and anxiously awaited his report.

"Well, I've checked the house from top to bottom. There are some minor fixes needed but no major issues to be concerned about," he said. "However, there are a few electrical outlets that should be replaced because they are very old and outdated."

He told Mom that he would send her a written report and noticed her look of concern.

"Hey, don't worry! No house is perfect," he reassured her. "Many homes need some kind of repair. Once the outlets are updated, this house will be safe for you and Mackie."

***

Later that evening, Mrs. Holmes shared the inspection report with Mom. There were several minor repairs that needed to be done, but Mom agreed they were things that she could tackle over time. However, she was concerned that the outdated electrical outlets may be unsafe.

Mrs. Holmes took Mom's concerns to Mrs. Robinson who agreed to have the old outlets checked and updated by an **electrician**. Mom breathed a huge sigh of relief.

CHAPTER 10
The BIG Oops!

The Closing day was a couple of weeks away. Mom felt this was the perfect time to get rid of stuff they no longer needed and to prepare for their move. Mackie boxed up the clothes she had outgrown and the toys she no longer played with to donate to a local charity. The charity would offer the items in their warehouse Free Store for those in need.

The donation pickup crew from Free Store arrived bright and early Saturday morning. Mackie was away at a sleepover, so Mom taped the boxes Mackie had prepared to give away. The crew quickly loaded all the boxes and gave Mom a charitable donation receipt. This receipt shared the value of the items she donated to get credit for her contribution on her tax return.

***

Later that day, Mackie returned from her sleepover and saw that all the donation boxes had been removed from her room. She immediately noticed the box of toys was missing. Mackie frantically searched her entire room for the tiara she had thrown in the box months before. She looked in the special tiara box, but it was empty. She looked under the bed. She looked in the closet. She rifled through every dresser drawer. NO TIARA!

Her room looked as if a cyclone had torn through it. The tiara was GONE! "MOM-MMMMMMMM!!!!!" Mackie shrieked at the top of her voice. "I can't find the princess crown Daddy gave me!" She remembered the day she threw it onto the toy box when Mom said she couldn't decorate her room. But the tiara was a special treasure from her father and she just had to find it.

"Mom, PLEASE tell me you moved my tiara!" Mackie pointed to the empty space beside her dresser where the box once sat. "I left it right here on top of the box that was next to my dresser. Now, the whole box is gone!"

"Oh, no!" Mom's heart sank. "The donation truck came today and I must have mistakenly given them the wrong box. Princess, I am SO sorry! If we hurry, maybe we can make it to Free Store in time to get it back." Mom tried to sound hopeful. She knew how much the tiara meant to Mackie.

Mackie was in tears all the way. "Mommy, we MUST get my tiara back! Daddy would be so disappointed in me right now."

"Honey, don't be so hard on yourself. If your dad were here he would tell you that we should give ourselves and others grace when mistakes happen."

Mom gave Mackie a tight and reassuring hug then they hurried out the door in hopes of making it there before closing. They arrived just as the shop clerk was locking the door and lowering the window shade. Mackie ran up to the door and began to pound on the glass. The

startled clerk turned and saw Mackie's worried face and hurried to unlock the door.

"Excuse me, miss," Mackie uttered with tears running down her cheeks, "my daddy gave me a special gift and now it's gone. My daddy is..." Mackie's mom carefully stroked Mackie's hair to calm her down a bit, then turned to the clerk.

"Ma'am, I accidentally donated a very special tiara that belongs to my daughter. You see, her father gave it to her a short time before he passed away. We were hoping you could find it and return it to us. It would have come in on a truck earlier today. It has very colorful jewels on the outside and a special inscription on the inside."

"I know exactly the tiara you're speaking of. It came in this morning. We all admired how stunning it was." The clerk had a worried look on her face. "But I'm so sorry to have to tell you that it didn't stay on the shelf very long. Someone came in and placed it in their cart. The woman said it would be the perfect gift for a special little girl."

"Well, can you call her and explain that it's mine and I must get it back?" Mackie asked as she tried to hold back another flood of tears.

"I really wish I could help you, sweetie, but we have no way to contact customers." The clerk placed her hands over her heart while she looked down at Mackie. "I am so sorry, dear… so very sorry!"

Mackie and Mom were devastated. Mackie felt that she had completely let her father down. The tiara was the only connection she had to her father and now it was gone, forever.

Mackie sobbed the entire drive home. "Princess, I'm so sorry your beautiful tiara is gone, but remember that you still have that picture of you and your dad on your seventh birthday when you were wearing your tiara. You have many great memories of your tiara and time spent with your father. He will always be alive in your heart and mind."

"I know, Mommy," said Mackie between sniffles, "it's just that, every time I wore my princess crown, it made me think of all the good times with Dad and my pinky promise to him to never stop dreaming."

That night, when Mackie knelt beside her bed to say her bedtime prayers, her mother overheard the sweetest most sincere prayer:

Dear God, I am so sorry for not being more responsible with my gift. If I ever get it back, I will treasure it forever. But if I NEVER get it back...I pray my crown will make another little girl feel special like it did for me, and that she will cherish it as much as I did.

Oh! and God? Can you please tell my daddy that I love him and I miss him?

Oh! And let him know that I will never stop dreaming like I promised.

Amen.

CHAPTER 11
The BIG Appraisal

After the home inspection was finished and the **seller** completed the requested repairs, Mom felt comfortable moving forward with the home purchase. Mrs. Lopez, the loan officer, ordered an **appraisal** for the house. She explained to Mackie and Mom that the lender would only allow homebuyers to borrow what the home is worth, so they hired an appraiser to determine its value.

***

Later that day, Mackie sat on the front stoop of her apartment gazing across the street at the beautiful castle house. She noticed a car turning into the driveway. The driver reached into her back seat to get a camera and clipboard.

Mackie watched intently as the woman walked and took some photos of two other houses on the block. *This must be the appraiser Mrs. Lopez told them about*, Mackie thought. The woman noticed Mackie, then smiled and waved.

Mackie jumped to her feet and began running to the edge of the curb to wave back. "Hi," she shouted in her loudest voice. "My name is Mackenzie, but everybody calls me Mac—" All of a sudden, she slipped and fell into the grass. The appraiser hurried across the street to make sure Mackie was okay.

"Oh, my! Are you okay, Dear?" she asked while helping Mackie to her feet.

"Yes, ma'am, I'm fine. My name is Mackenzie, but everybody calls me Mackie," she replied as she attempted to brush the grass stains from her knees. "You're the appraiser, aren't you?"

The appraiser looked very surprised. "Why, yes, I am an appraiser." She paused then asked with a puzzled look on her face, "How could you possibly know that?"

"Welllll, my mommy and I are buying this castle house and Mrs. Lopez said an appraiser would stop by to make sure the house is worth every dollar we are paying for it."

"You are a very smart young lady! That's exactly what I'm here to do. My name is Hiroko Chang, but everyone calls me HC."

"Miss HC, what a cool name! But I thought an appraiser would be a man."

Sensing Mackie's curiosity, Miss HC explained, "That's okay. Unfortunately, there are very few women in this career. Can you believe I am the only woman appraiser in our entire city? I really love appraising properties and I would love to see more bright young ladies like yourself in this field. If I can do it, so can you!" Mackie noticed how Miss HC's face lit up as she talked about her job.

"I have the coolest career. I get to spend my days visiting all types of homes and buildings all around the city. Every building is unique.

"I drive all over town. I also research each home on the internet to discover and learn as much information as I can about the prop-

erties I appraise. Then I compare what the other houses sold for in the neighborhood to determine how much it is worth."

"That sounds like a lot of work!" Mackie said.

"It's very important that I collect as much data as I can to make sure the report is accurate. When I finish here today, I will write a report that includes my professional opinion of the value of the home. Then I will send it to Mrs. Lopez at the bank. She will review my report and contact you if the appraised value is acceptable." Miss HC glanced at her watch, "Oh! How time flies...I'd better get back to my work!"

Mackie watched as Miss HC snapped photos and took notes on the forms on her clipboard. She enjoyed talking with Miss HC and was very impressed.

"If you and your mom ever have questions about appraisals you can call me. And if you ever want to experience a day in the life of an appraiser, I would love to have you both tag along." Miss HC handed her business card to Mackie.

"That sounds fun! It was very nice meeting

you, Miss HC."

"It was my pleasure, Miss Mackie."

Miss HC walked back toward the house to finish her appraisal while Mackie walked back to sit on her apartment steps. When Miss HC finished taking photos of the inside of the house, she waved goodbye to Mackie. Mackie rushed up the stairs to show her mom the business card and to tell her all about Miss HC.

Later that week, Mrs. Lopez called with the news that the home appraised well and their mortgage loan was officially approved. "Congratulations! We can now schedule your closing," she said.

The two soon-to-be-homeowners did their happy dance all around the apartment. Mackie snatched the checklist from under the magnet on the refrigerator door and checked the steps off their list.

STEP 6: Have a Home Inspection.

STEP 7: Get an Appraisal.

CHAPTER 12
The BIG Dream Team

It was FINALLY closing day! Mom picked Mackie up from school then rushed to the bank to withdraw a **cashier's check** from the 'Castle Fund' for the down payment and closing costs. They arrived in the nick of time for their 3 o'clock closing appointment at the **title office**.

Once inside the title office, Mom began to fiddle with the pen in her left hand. She kept looking at the cashier's check to make sure the amount was correct. She had already given Mrs. Ollie, the landlord, her moving notice. There was no turning back now! She was excited, nervous, and terrified all at the same time.

At that very moment, she glanced downwards

and her eyes locked with Mackie's. She saw the future in her daughter's small round face. Suddenly, she felt a sense of peace. She smiled, took a deep breath, lifted her head high, and walked into the meeting room hand in hand with her little princess.

As they sat around a long oval-shaped wooden conference table, Mackie smiled at the familiar faces. Mrs. Holmes (the real estate agent), Mrs. Lopez (the mortgage loan officer), Mr. Collins (the homeownership specialist), and Mrs. Robinson (the seller), all chatted with Mackie and Mom about how excited they were for them to have a new house.

Interestingly, there was one person Mackie and Mom had yet to meet—Mr. Rome, the **title officer**. His job was to handle the closing by making sure all the documents were signed properly by the buyer and the seller. Mr. Rome was quite a character! His great sense of humor was only magnified by his wonderful laugh. All sorts of funny stories and corny jokes filled the room. Without missing a beat, he fit right into the team by making Mackie and Mom laugh, which helped Mom feel at ease.

Mrs. Holmes

Mrs. Lopez

Mr. Collins

Mrs. Robin

Mackie

Mom

Mr. Rome

81

Mackie looked around the table, and in true Mackie fashion, announced, "I'm going to call you all 'The Dream Team' because you are all helping to make our dream come true!" Everyone smiled and nodded in agreement. They liked that nickname!

"Mackenzie, your job is to keep a count of each time your mother signs her name," Mr. Rome said as he began sifting through the huge stack of papers for Mom and Mrs. Robinson to sign. Mr. Rome knew this was a life-changing moment for Mom, but also knew how boring closings could be for kids. He wanted to keep Mackie entertained during the process.

Halfway through the signing, Mr. Rome asked Mackie for an official signature count. "Um, maybe 30?" she guessed while looking at her counting fingers and hunching her shoulders. She giggled and admitted she had lost count long ago.

Finally, they were down to the final document. The **deed**. "This is the most important document of the entire closing," Mr. Rome said. "This little piece of paper officially transfers the house to you and Mackenzie."

After Mrs. Robinson signed the deed, Mr. Rome turned to Mackie and said, "Congratulations, YOU JUST BOUGHT A HOUSE!"

Mackie started clapping, which prompted everyone else to clap and cheer along. Mr. Rome reached into the recycle bin and pulled out handfuls of shredded paper. He passed a couple of fistfuls to Mackie, and they threw them in the air like confetti.

After the celebration settled a bit, Mrs. Robinson walked over to Mom and gave her a warm smile and handed over the keys to the castle house. "I prayed that a good family would buy my home...and God has surely answered my prayers."

She turned toward Mackie, bent down, and said, "Hello, Princess Mackie, it's very nice to finally meet you." Mrs. Robinson handed Mackie a small gold key. "My daughter, Naomi, asked me to give you this key. It unlocks a special box she left in your new room."

Mackie's eyes grew wide with surprise and wonder. Her hands clasped around the gold key and she opened her arms wide to give Mrs.

Robinson a great big hug. "Oh, thank you. Thank you! Thank you sooooo much for letting us buy your castle!" she exclaimed gleefully while holding tightly onto Mrs. Robinson.

The Dream Team gave their best wishes to Mackie and Mom for their new home and said their goodbyes. When they got into the car, Mackie pulled the checklist from her backpack. Together they checked off:

STEP 8: Closing Day!

CHAPTER 13
The BIG Move!

The next morning, the two brand new home owners woke up with the sun. They began to pack a few small boxes of last-minute items before the movers arrived. Suddenly, it hit Mackie that she was standing in the bedroom of the apartment where she had spent her entire life. After today, she would have a new room with new memories. Tears began to cloud the vision of herself in the mirror.

She looked at her father's picture on her wall and felt sad that he was not here to celebrate this big moment with them. She felt as if she was, somehow, leaving him behind. Then she noticed the empty box that once safely guarded

her precious tiara. Her father wanted her to wear that tiara when she finally got her castle. Now it was gone forever.

It hurt Mom's heart to see Mackie struggling with such sadness. She hugged her tightly and reminded her of how proud her father would be of them on this joyous day. Mackie nodded her head and wiped a tear before carefully lifting her father's picture from the wall and placing it carefully inside the tiara box. Once everything was gone from her room, she turned out the light and closed her bedroom door for the last time.

Mackie examined every room in the apartment and remembered the many good times spent there with family and friends. She slowly walked down the stairs and hugged Mr. and Mrs. Ollie who stood on the porch to say their goodbyes. "I'm really going to miss hearing you bounce down those stairs, Mackie," Mrs. Ollie said, and handed Mackie a tin full of her delicious homemade cookies. Mr. Ollie hugged his wife who he saw was about to cry.

"I'll be right across the street. I will still stop by for your famous cookies all the time," Mackie said as she waved and got into the back seat of the car. She held her small box on her lap and said, "All set, Mommy."

They drove the car directly across the street and into the driveway of their new home while singing and wiggling in their seats, "We bought a hooou-ouse, we bought a hooou-ouse."

Before they got out of the car, Mackie pulled the tattered checklist from her backpack for the last time. They both glanced over the checklist and all the checkmarks. "Wow, we've done a lot of hard work, Mackie. We only have one more box to check."

They both exclaimed in unison:

"STEP 9: MOVE-IN...CHECK!"

The two hopped out of the car, grabbed the boxes from the back seat, and rushed to open the front door. Mackie could not wait another second to find out what the special key was for. She dashed up the never-ending staircase, down the long hallway past the bathroom and the "boring-blah-blue" bedroom. She was eager to discover what treasure the key would unlock

☑ Step 1: Save Money for Your **Down Payment**

☑ Step 2: Get Pre-Approved for a **Mortgage**

☑ Step 3: Find the right **Real Estate Agent**

☑ Step 4: Shop for the Right House.

☑ Step 5: Make an Offer

☑ Step 6: Have a **Home Inspection**

☑ Step 7: Get a Home **Appraisal**

☑ Step 8: Closing Day!

☑ Step 9: MOVE IN!!! CONGRATULATIONS! You're a Homeowner!

inside her "Perfect Princess Room."

She pushed open her heavy creaky bedroom door that brushed across the carpet. There, on the bed, was a sparkly envelope on top of a box wrapped with a big oversized pink bow.

Dear Princess Mackie,
My name is Naomi, and this was once my room. When I was about your age, my mom and dad called me a Princess, too. My mom even helped me decorate my room so it would be perfect for a princess. I left everything the same for you. I hope you love it. I also left you a special gift inside the box.

Mackie carefully put the letter down and began to pull the strands of the pink bow on the box. She slowly unlocked the box with the special key and lifted the top. A burst of baby rainbows glistened on her beautiful carmel-colored face. Mackie's jaw dropped open. She couldn't believe her eyes.

It was THE princess tiara from her father! The ornate, colorful, jewel and gem-covered tiara glimmered in the box. It was Naomi who had gone to donate items from her mom's house as she moved and noticed the tiara on the shelf of the shop. She had no idea it originally belonged to Mackie.

Mackie held up the tiara and read:

"Dear Princess, You can do anything you put your mind to...Never Stop Dreaming! Love Always, Dad."

With the biggest smile on her face and tears of joy in her eyes, Mackie continued reading the letter from Naomi

When I first laid eyes on this tiara, I knew it was the perfect gift for you. It was as if it was made especially for you. I hope it brings you joy. Every time you wear this tiara, I want you to remember that you, Miss Mackie, are royalty. You have always been, and will always be, a Strong, Smart, and Beautiful Princess.

You never gave up on your dream to own a Castle, and you deserve this special crown.

Love,
Queen Naomi

PS. This castle is just the beginning of the empire you will build.

Mackie walked over to her new bedroom mirror, looked at herself for a moment, and gently placed the tiara around her perfect crinkly ponytail puffs. She thought about everything she had learned during the long journey, not only about buying a home, but about herself. She was strong. She was courageous. She was powerful. For the very first time, Mackie truly understood what it meant to be a real Princess.

Mom walked into the room and was stunned to see Mackie reunited with her beautiful tiara. She couldn't believe her eyes. She looked toward heaven and mouthed, "Thank you!" Happy tears began to settle in her eyes.

"Now, there's my Princess," Mom said. "I just want to thank you for helping me believe that we could buy this home. I must admit, this is the scariest thing I have ever done, but we did it. Always remember that you can do ANYTHING you set your mind to, no matter how big or how scary it may seem. Everything you need is already inside of you."

Mackie turned and curtsied. "You're welcome, Your Highness." The two laughed.

"I hope you can handle ONE more big surprise today," Mom said. "I was so touched that you used your puppy fund to help buy this house, so…" She motioned for Mackie to remove the blanket from the box in her arms. As Mackie began lifting the blanket, she heard paper rustling.

Mackie snatched off the blanket and squealed at the sight of the cutest, cuddliest puppy she had ever seen. She gently lifted her new friend from the box and snuggled him against her cheek. "Oh, Mommy! I LOVE him!! I'm going to name him Sir Maximillian. But we can call him Max, for short!"

She tossed herself across the bed and let Max jump and play with her. Mom joined in the fun and began to tickle Mackie and Max. Mackie wiggled and giggled as loud as she could. There was no one to complain about her loud singing or dancing anymore.

She sat up and hugged her mother tightly. "This is EXACTLY the way I dreamed it would feel, Mom. I knew we could do it.

At that very moment, Mackie decided that when she grew up, she would help other

princesses buy their own castles. And, with her sidekick Max along for every adventure, that is exactly what they did!

THE END

A Message From

amerifirst® HOME MORTGAGE

Praise About Princess Mackie Buys a House

Owning the roof over your head has long been part of the American dream. It remains one of the fastest ways to build wealth and achieve economic security. Buying a home can be daunting, but even the seasoned professionals started out as first-time homebuyers! Just like any journey, it begins with the first step. You should know that you don't have to go it alone. As Mackie discovers, no matter what community you're in, there are resources available to get you started.

For years, our company has worked alongside Twala Lockett-Jones to expand homeownership in places like her hometown of Kalamazoo, Michigan. We also work to educate families and improve financial literacy. That's why we were so excited to read *Princess Mackie Buys a House*. Teachers rarely discuss homeownership in the classroom. Therefore, the duty often falls on practitioners to get the word out. We need more works like *Princess Mackie Buys a House* to deliver that message to students across America, to educate the next generation and empower them to take command of their financial future.

Twala Lockett-Jones has 25 years of experience in real estate, community engagement, and passion for educating youth. She presents this message of homeownership in a way that resonates with youth. We couldn't be more proud to partner with Twala on this important effort and are so thankful to have her in our community.

Mark A. Jones
Co-Founder and CEO | Amerifirst Home Mortgage
Vice Chairman | Mortgage Bankers Association of America

About the Author

Twala Lockett-Jones fell in love with real estate (and chocolate) as a young child. She bought her first house when she was only 19 years old and it sparked a passion to buy even more. Today, she and her husband Kenneth have purchased more than 40 homes. They enjoy fixing up old, neglected houses to beautify their community.

Mrs. Lockett-Jones turned her passion into a profession when she became a Realtor in 1996. She loves helping new homeowners, and she realizes homeownership is a BIG DEAL! In 2019, she became a real estate broker and opened Lockett-Jones Realty Group. During her career in real estate, she has helped more than 1,000 princesses (and their families) find their dream castles.

Twala and her husband live in Kalamazoo, Michigan. They have 3 grown children…and she still eats lots of chocolate!

About the Illustrator

Melissa Bailey is an award-winning illustrator, author, and smiley person. (Seriously. She smiles all the time.) She's also an avid reader, averaging over 600 children's books a year. (Yes. She counted.)

Melissa has illustrated over 50 books, including *Steve the Dung Beetle* (which won the 2019 Moonbeam Awards silver medal for Best Illustrator). She is the author-illustrator of two books: *Pug Is Happy* (2018) and *Imara's Tiara* (2020, co-written with Susan R. Stoltz), both published by Pygmy Giraffe Publishing. A member of SCBWI since 2013, she volunteers as a self-publishing advisor in her region.

When she's not in her studio splashing paint or typing away at her keyboard, she's probably outside walking her poodles, who demand three walks a day. If it's too dark for walks, she might be cooking (and eating), binging old TV shows, drawing, or avoiding doing the dishes. (If only poodles could be trained to wash dishes…)

You can contact Melissa via her website (mbaileyart. com) or follow her on Instagram (@mbaileyart). She'd love to hear from you!

GLOSSARY

Appraisal - An appraisal is a report estimating the value of a home.

Borrow - To take and use money with the promise of paying it back.

Budget - A budget is a written plan for how you save and/or spend money. A budget tells your money where to go and what to do.

Buyer's Agent - The Buyer's Agent is a real estate agent who works for the buyer. They will show homes to the buyer and guide the buyer throughout the homebuying process.

Cashier's Check - A cashier's check is a safe way to make large payments. The check is written by a bank or credit union.

Close/Closing - The closing is a meeting where all final paperwork involved in the home purchase are signed.

Closing Costs - Closing costs include a variety of fees paid for at the closing for the purchase of a home, such as taxes, insurance, and title work. Most closing costs are paid by the buyer, but the seller covers some.

Contractor - A contractor is a person who gets paid to perform work on a house.

Credit Report - A credit report is a record of your credit history. A credit report includes information about the amount and type of credit used, how much you owe, and how well you pay back money you borrowed.

Credit Score - Your credit score is a number ranging from 300 to 850 that's based on your credit history. This number can be found on your credit report.

Deed - A piece of paper that shows who owns a house.

Down Payment - A down payment is a portion of the total home price paid in one lump sum at the closing. The higher the down payment, the smaller the amount of the mortgage loan needed to pay for the home.

Electrician - An Electrician works with electrical power. They install and repair wiring in houses, such as lights and outlets.

Equity - Equity refers to the portion of the home's value that belongs to the homeowner, rather than the bank. As the homeowner pays down the mortgage, and the value of the home rises over time, the equity increases.

Generational Wealth - Generational wealth refers to any kind of asset that families pass down to their children or grandchildren. It can be in the form of cash, investment funds, stocks and bonds, houses or even businesses.

Interest Rate - The interest rate is the amount the lender charges you for borrowing money and is a percentage of the amount borrowed.

Home Inspection - A home inspection is conducted on behalf of the buyer during the homebuying process. During the home inspection, the inspector will check the condition of the home, from the plumbing and electrical systems to the foundation. The inspector will then provide a full home report about the condition of the home.

Landlord - A landlord is a person who owns a house and rents it out to other people.

Lender - A lender is a bank, credit union, or mortgage company that loans money to people. The lender expects to be paid back over time.

Mortgage - A mortgage is a special type of loan used to buy a house. Most people don't have the cash to buy a house, so they borrow money from a bank, credit union or mortgage company.

Negotiate - To bargain or come to an agreement with another person.

Offer - This is the amount of money offered for a home by a buyer. The buyer's offer is written on a purchase agreement.

Pre-Approval Letter - Before beginning the home search, a buyer needs a pre-approval letter which shows how much a bank will lend them. The bank will determine how much it is willing to lend based on the buyer's income and credit.

Profit - The amount of money made by selling something for more than the amount paid for it.

Purchase Agreement - A written contract between a buyer and a seller to purchase a home.

Seller's Agent - The Seller's Agent is a real estate agent who prices the home, markets the home for sale and helps the seller with other aspects of selling the home.

Showing - A showing is a private tour of a home set up for a buyer by their real estate agent.

Tenant - A Tenant is a person who pays rent to live in a home that is owned by someone else.

Title Office/Title Company - The Title Office or Title Company works on behalf of both the lender and the buyer. You hire them to research and insure the title of the home you're buying.

Victorian Home - Victorian Homes are a style of house named for the era Queen Victoria reigned in Great Britain from 1837 to 1901. The fancy designs of Queen Anne Victorian homes look similar to castles and dollhouses.